Quiz 153311
8.6

SUMMER OLYMPIC LEGENDS

GYMNASTICS

BY NATE LeBOUTILLIER

CREATIVE 🍎 EDUCATION

GYMNASTICS

CONTENTS

Throughout human history, people have always sought to challenge themselves, to compete against others, and to discover the limits of their capabilities. Such desires can turn destructive, leading to war. But the ancient Greeks also recognized the good in these human traits, and it was because of them that the Olympic Games—featuring running races, jumping contests, throwing competitions, and wrestling and boxing matches—began more than 2,700 years ago. The ancient Olympics ended in A.D. 393, but the Games were revived in 1896 in hopes of promoting world peace through sports. Fittingly, the first "modern" Olympics were held in Athens, Greece, but they moved around the world every four years after that. In 2009, it was announced that the Games would be held in South America for the first time, going to Rio de Janeiro, Brazil, in 2016.

Every 1896 Olympian received a medal reading "International Olympic Games, Athens 1896"

Gymnastics, a set of exercises showcasing athletes' strength, agility, balance, and gracefulness, was practiced by the ancient Greeks and Romans. In more modern times, the sport was revived in Germany in the early 1800s as a movement called *Turnverein*. Much of the credit for this movement went to physical educators Friedrich Jahn, known as the "Father of Gymnastics" in Germany, and Johann GutsMuths, who wrote *Gymnastik für die Jugend* (*Gymnastics for Youth*), a textbook that showed how to work gymnastics into school curriculum. By the time the first modern Olympics were held in 1896, athletes all across Europe were participating in gymnastics, so the sport was featured in the Games of Athens. Indeed, gymnastics is one of just five sports (the others being swimming, track and field, cycling, and fencing) that have appeared in every modern Olympiad.

Featuring events that demand a wide range of physical maneuvers—from demonstrations of extreme upper-body power to near impossible body arches to aerial flips and spins—gymnastics has long been among the Olympics' most popular competitions. And the sport has produced its share of legendary athletes and classic moments. From America's George Eyser to Romania's Nadia Comaneci to China's Yang Wei, gymnasts—male and female—have thrilled sports fans for more than a century. And although gymnastics has also faced low points in the form of apparatus problems and judging controversies, such incidents have added their own unforgettable moments to the history of this elegant Olympic sport.

A stamp honoring German Friedrich Jahn, famed for his many contributions to gymnastics

ATHENS, GREECE · 1896
PARIS, FRANCE · 1900
ST. LOUIS, MISSOURI · 1904
LONDON, ENGLAND · 1908
STOCKHOLM, SWEDEN · 1912
ANTWERP, BELGIUM · 1920
PARIS, FRANCE · 1924
AMSTERDAM, NETHERLANDS · 1928
LOS ANGELES, CALIFORNIA · 1932
BERLIN, GERMANY · 1936
LONDON, ENGLAND · 1948
HELSINKI, FINLAND · 1952
MELBOURNE, AUSTRALIA · 1956
ROME, ITALY · 1960
TOKYO, JAPAN · 1964
MEXICO CITY, MEXICO · 1968
MUNICH, WEST GERMANY · 1972
MONTREAL, QUEBEC · 1976
MOSCOW, SOVIET UNION · 1980
LOS ANGELES, CALIFORNIA · 1984
SEOUL, SOUTH KOREA · 1988
BARCELONA, SPAIN · 1992
ATLANTA, GEORGIA · 1996
SYDNEY, AUSTRALIA · 2000
ATHENS, GREECE · 2004
BEIJING, CHINA · 2008
LONDON, ENGLAND · 2012

GOLD, SILVER, BRONZE, AND WOOD

1904 ST. LOUIS, MISSOURI

Some details of the life of Olympic gymnast George Eyser are unknown. What is known is that Eyser was born in 1871 in Kiel, Germany, and that he lost his left leg as a child after being hit by a train. Eyser emigrated to the United States with his family in 1885 and gained American citizenship in 1894. Eventually, he made his way to St. Louis, where he found work as a bookkeeper for a construction company. It is also known that Eyser was not only a gymnastics participant at the 1904 St. Louis Games, but he was a medalist as well. In fact, he was one of the Olympics' greatest early champions, winning medals—three of them gold—in six different events.

George Eyser (center), pictured in 1908 as a member of the American Concordia Turnverein club

The 1904 Olympiad was not a perfectly run event. St. Louis tied the Games to its own World's Fair and held events from July to November—an oddly extended schedule that contributed to low attendance by both participants and spectators. Writer Charles J. P. Lucas bemoaned the scant participation in his book *The Olympic Games 1904, St. Louis*, noting that "England and France did not send a single competitor to America, and the French people showed their ingratitude by an entire absence of representation. America made the Paris Games of 1900 a success, and without American entries the second revival of the Games would have been a farce." The Olympic gymnastics competition was representative of the larger problems of the St. Louis Games, as gymnasts from just three nations participated. Of the 119 total participants, a whopping 111 were American, 7 were German, and 1 was Swiss.

Eyser put the 118 other gymnasts in his shadow. On October 29, he won all six of his medals in a single day. He won the rope climb event in a great show of upper-body strength by clambering up 25 feet of rope in 7.2 seconds, just edging out American Charles Krause, who ascended the same distance in 7.4 seconds. Eyser also captured gold in the parallel bars and then tied American Anton Heida for first in the "long horse" vault. Eyser's vault was particularly impressive, considering he had to pick up adequate speed on the runway to the vault while sprinting on one wooden leg. Eyser also won a silver medal in the pommel horse and combined events, as well as a bronze in the horizontal bar.

After the Olympic Games of 1904, Eyser continued to compete with the American Concordia Turnverein gymnastics club, which won top honors at an international competition in Germany in 1908 as well as the championship of the National Turnfest gymnastics competition in Cincinnati, Ohio, in 1909. From there, the details of Eyser's life grow sketchy; his whereabouts in the following years and the date and place of his death remain unknown. His legendary Olympic performance, however, was evoked more than 100 years later when South African swimmer Natalie du Toit garnered fanfare by finishing 16th in the 10-kilometer swimming event in the 2008 Olympics in Beijing, China, despite swimming with only one leg, having lost the other in a motorized scooter accident.

ATHENS, GREECE | PARIS, FRANCE | ST. LOUIS, MISSOURI | LONDON, ENGLAND | STOCKHOLM, SWEDEN | ANTWERP, BELGIUM | PARIS, FRANCE | AMSTERDAM, NETHERLANDS | LOS ANGELES, CALIFORNIA | BERLIN, GERMANY | LONDON, ENGLAND | HELSINKI, FINLAND | MELBOURNE, AUSTRALIA | ROME, ITALY | TOKYO, JAPAN | MEXICO CITY, MEXICO | MUNICH, WEST GERMANY | MONTREAL, QUEBEC | MOSCOW, SOVIET UNION | LOS ANGELES, CALIFORNIA | SEOUL, SOUTH KOREA | BARCELONA, SPAIN | ATLANTA, GEORGIA | SYDNEY, AUSTRALIA | ATHENS, GREECE | BEIJING, CHINA | LONDON, ENGLAND

1896 | 1900 | 1904 | 1908 | 1912 | 1920 | 1924 | 1928 | 1932 | 1936 | 1948 | 1952 | 1956 | 1960 | 1964 | 1968 | 1972 | 1976 | 1980 | 1984 | 1988 | 1992 | 1996 | 2000 | 2004 | 2008 | 2012

THE LOST APPARATUS

ROPE CLIMBING & INDIAN CLUBS

Since 1936, Olympic medals in gymnastics have been awarded to competitors in 10 standard categories: team, individual all-around, floor exercise, vault, horizontal bar (men only), parallel bars (men), pommel horse (men), rings (men), balance beam (women only), and uneven bars

Sailors in England's Royal Navy included Indian clubs as part of their training in the 1930s

(women). Before that, though, two other events for men—rope climbing and Indian clubs—made brief but memorable appearances in the arenas of Olympic competition.

Athletic rope climbing dates back to the ancient Greeks and Romans, who trained soldiers with the climbing of ropes. German educator Friedrich Jahn wrote in his 1816 book *Die Deutsche Turnkunst* (*The German Gymnastic Art*) that the most difficult type of rope climbing is that done with "both feet and only one hand," while also noting, "it is not easy to climb upside down." Four times, from the first modern Olympics in Athens in 1896 through the Olympics of 1932 in Los Angeles, rope climbing was a certified part of the gymnastics program for men.

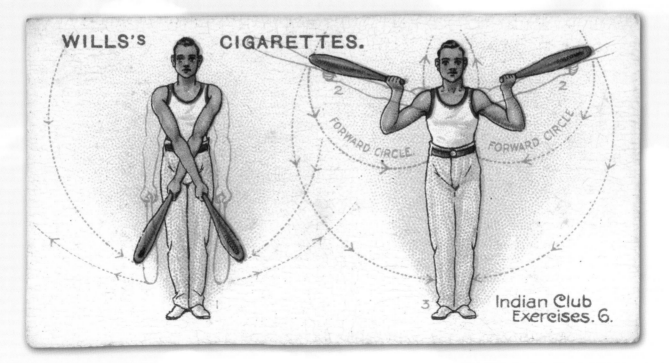

This diagram from the early 1900s depicts the precise movements involved in using Indian clubs

Rope climbers in Athens were judged on both speed and style as they scrambled up a rope some 14 meters in length, and Greek gymnast Nikolaos Andriakopoulos won that first modern Olympic rope climb. The next Olympic champion rope climber was German-American George Eyser in 1904. Eyser famously collected gold medals in three different gymnastics categories in St. Louis, though rope climbing was considered his forte due to the combination of his supreme upper-body strength and the fact that he had a wooden left leg, which reduced his overall body weight. Czechoslovakian Bedrich Supcik edged out Frenchman Albert Seguin at the Paris Games of 1924 before rope climbing made its final Olympic appearance in Los Angeles in 1932, when U.S. Naval Academy graduate Benny Bass took gold by ascending an 8-meter rope in just 6.7 seconds. Rope climbing was discontinued as an Olympic event after artistic gymnasts complained that it was more of a track and field activity. But track and field, it seemed, had no use for the rope climb in its program of events, so the rope disappeared.

Indian clubs were a fascinating gymnastics apparatus for men featured in both the 1904 and 1932 Games. Grasping a pair of clubs that were roughly the shape and size of bowling pins, a competitor would seem to nearly juggle the clubs, though in actuality the clubs never left his hands and were swung in carefully choreographed patterns about the head and body. The use of Indian clubs as a means of exercise became popular in the late 1800s in both Europe and America, but the clubs originated in India, where they were used in conjunction with a sort of nationalistic wrestling program. The first Indian clubs Olympic champion was American Edward Hennig, who scored a judges' rating of 13 (on an unspecified scale) to beat runners-up Emil Voigt and Ralph Wilson, also Americans, who had earned scores of 9 and 5 respectively. In 1932, the champion Indian club swinger was American George Roth. After receiving his gold medal in front of 60,000 Olympic spectators, Roth, who was unemployed at the time, walked out of the stadium and hitchhiked home.

In Olympic rope climbing, athletes began their climb from a seated position and ascended using only their hands and arms, though rhythmic leg kicking was permitted.

ATHENS, GREECE 1896
PARIS, FRANCE 1900
ST. LOUIS, MISSOURI 1904
LONDON, ENGLAND 1908
STOCKHOLM, SWEDEN 1912
ANTWERP, BELGIUM 1920
PARIS, FRANCE 1924
AMSTERDAM, NETHERLANDS 1928
LOS ANGELES, CALIFORNIA 1932
BERLIN, GERMANY 1936
LONDON, ENGLAND 1948
HELSINKI, FINLAND 1952
MELBOURNE, AUSTRALIA 1956
ROME, ITALY 1960
TOKYO, JAPAN 1964
MEXICO CITY, MEXICO 1968
MUNICH, WEST GERMANY 1972
MONTREAL, QUEBEC 1976
MOSCOW, SOVIET UNION 1980
LOS ANGELES, CALIFORNIA 1984
SEOUL, SOUTH KOREA 1988
BARCELONA, SPAIN 1992
ATLANTA, GEORGIA 1996
SYDNEY, AUSTRALIA 2000
ATHENS, GREECE 2004
BEIJING, CHINA 2008
LONDON, ENGLAND 2012

FOR THE MOTHERLAND

LARISSA LATYNINA SOVIET UNION OLYMPIC COMPETITIONS: 1956, 1960, 1964

Out of the "Soviet Sports Machine"—a nationalistic athletic program created to restore pride and bring glory to the Soviet Union following World War II (1939–45)—came one of the most dominant Olympic athletes of all time: gymnast Larissa Latynina.

Larissa Latynina, pictured with one of her gold medals won during the 1960 Summer Olympics

Latynina first competed at the 1956 Olympics in Melbourne, Australia. There, she engaged in a rivalry with Hungarian gymnast Agnes Keleti, who had won four medals in Helsinki, Finland, in 1952. While Keleti won gold in uneven bars, balance beam, and floor exercise in Melbourne, Latynina won gold in the vault, floor exercise (tie), and individual all-around competitions. She also captured gold with her Soviet compatriots in the team competition. The overall Olympic medal board, meanwhile, was also dominated by the Soviet Union for the first time. In all, Latynina won six medals in Melbourne, and she perfectly fit the bill of the stereotypical Soviet athlete of the time with her stoic demeanor, no-nonsense approach, and intense will to win. "Oh, I was a very big patriot," Latynina said later in life. "My gymnastics was not only mine. It belonged to my Soviet motherland and all the people."

Latynina was just as impressive at the next Olympics, held in 1960 in Rome, Italy. Again, Latynina collected six medals overall, three of them gold—including the coveted individual all-around for a second straight Olympiad. In 1964, Latynina, then 29 years of age—quite old for a sport that demands the flexibility of youth—pulled off the seemingly impossible, winning six medals in a single Games for a third time. As of 2012, her 18 Olympic medals were more than any other Olympian had earned. After the 1964 Games, Latynina turned to coaching, often prodding and overtraining young athletes to win glory for their country in the same way that she had been pushed.

In the 1976 Olympics in Montreal, Quebec, a young Romanian gymnast named Nadia Comaneci won the all-around women's gymnastics champion-ship. When Latynina returned home with her squad—which had won gold in the team competition—her country's sports committee dressed her down because a Soviet had failed to win all-around gold. "Comaneci deserved to win," said

Latynina padded her Olympic haul with silver (1960) and bronze (1964) medals on the balance beam

Latynina. "But the sports committee acted like I'd committed some deadly sin because we lost. They said I was outdated, obsolete." After having dedicated her entire life to the sport of gymnastics and to her country, Latynina tendered her resignation as Olympic coach.

Latynina remained in the Soviet Union and played a large role in organizing the Olympic gymnastics competition held in Moscow in 1980.

But the intensity of her allegiance to her country waned as she measured the time and work she'd given the Soviet Union against the rewards it had returned. "I believed in our system," said Latynina. "I believed and believed and believed. Now, sadly, I don't anymore. I realize it was all cheap propaganda. We athletes used to call out to our people: 'Go forward.' Now, all my work and all my beliefs have left me with nothing. Absolutely nothing."

Female Soviet gymnasts were dominant at the 1960 Games, winning all three medals in the vault

ATHENS, GREECE	PARIS, FRANCE	ST. LOUIS, MISSOURI	LONDON, ENGLAND	STOCKHOLM, SWEDEN	ANTWERP, BELGIUM	PARIS, FRANCE	AMSTERDAM, NETHERLANDS	LOS ANGELES, CALIFORNIA	BERLIN, GERMANY	LONDON, ENGLAND	HELSINKI, FINLAND	MELBOURNE, AUSTRALIA	ROME, ITALY	TOKYO, JAPAN	MEXICO CITY, MEXICO	MUNICH, WEST GERMANY	MONTREAL, QUEBEC	MOSCOW, SOVIET UNION	LOS ANGELES, CALIFORNIA	SEOUL, SOUTH KOREA	BARCELONA, SPAIN	ATLANTA, GEORGIA	SYDNEY, AUSTRALIA	ATHENS, GREECE	BEIJING, CHINA	LONDON, ENGLAND
1896	1900	1904	1908	1912	1920	1924	1928	1932	1936	1948	1952	1956	1960	1964	1968	1972	1976	1980	1984	1988	1992	1996	2000	2004	2008	2012

PIGTAILS AND BACKFLIPS

OLGA KORBUT SOVIET UNION OLYMPIC COMPETITIONS: 1972, 1976

In 1972, the Soviet Union dominated the Munich Olympic Games, winning 99 medals—50 of them gold—to lead all countries. However, Soviet athletes were seen by many outsiders as cold, machinelike, and joyless, products of a grim, state-run sports program that overworked its athletes in the quest for world supremacy. A little gymnast named Olga Korbut did her best to change that perception.

Olga Korbut proudly displays her individual all-around gold medal in the 1972 Olympics

Korbut, born in the Soviet state of Bélarus, started training at age eight under the tutelage of coach Renald Knysh. They worked together to become true innovators of the sport of women's gymnastics, which, at the time, emphasized elegance over technical proficiency. While Korbut was indeed elegant, Knysh worked with her to emphasize the acrobatic technicalities of her routines first and foremost. And when, at age 17, the 4-foot-11 Korbut unveiled her routines—along with her smile—to the world at the 1972 Olympics, audiences fell in love with her. "Olga's spectacular moves have evolved slowly," said Knysh. "I am not interested in gold medals. Judges are usually slow in accepting innovation. What I am concerned with is how spectators react to Olga, and I try to get her to think the same way."

Perhaps most notable of all Korbut's innovative routines were her breathtaking backflips on the balance beam and uneven bars. While watching the young Soviet's backflips, American broadcaster Gordon Maddux exclaimed to television audiences, "I don't believe it! Give her an 11!"

The crowds in Munich seemed to agree, especially when the judges controversially scored Korbut's final uneven bars routine only a 9.8. Korbut's preliminary uneven bars routines had been filled with mistakes, one even being judged a low score of 7.5, sending the pigtailed Korbut to the sidelines in tears, which further humanized her to those watching. The audience whistled and jeered at the judges' 9.8 score, but the score stood, and Korbut took silver in the event rather than gold. Her creative routines were justly rewarded in other areas, though, as she captured gold in the balance beam and floor exercise as well as for her part in the team competition. In fact, her performances were arguably the highlight of an Olympics that was marred by violence (the shooting of kidnapped Israeli athletes and coaches by Palestinian terrorists) and controversy (the bizarre refereeing of the men's gold-medal basketball game).

Korbut was nicknamed "The Sparrow from Minsk" (a reference to her Bélarus hometown)

1896 ATHENS, GREECE
1900 PARIS, FRANCE
1904 ST. LOUIS, MISSOURI
1908 LONDON, ENGLAND
1912 STOCKHOLM, SWEDEN
1920 ANTWERP, BELGIUM
1924 PARIS, FRANCE
1928 AMSTERDAM, NETHERLANDS
1932 LOS ANGELES, CALIFORNIA
1936 BERLIN, GERMANY
1948 LONDON, ENGLAND
1952 HELSINKI, FINLAND
1956 MELBOURNE, AUSTRALIA
1960 ROME, ITALY
1964 TOKYO, JAPAN
1968 MEXICO CITY, MEXICO
1972 MUNICH, WEST GERMANY
1976 MONTREAL, QUBEC
1980 MOSCOW, SOVIET UNION
1984 LOS ANGELES, CALIFORNIA
1988 SEOUL, SOUTH KOREA
1992 BARCELONA, SPAIN
1996 ATLANTA, GEORGIA
2000 SYDNEY, AUSTRALIA
2004 ATHENS, GREECE
2008 BEIJING, CHINA
2012 LONDON, ENGLAND

NADIA'S 10

1976 MONTREAL, QUEBEC

The names of her breathless gymnastics moves sounded like the repertoire of a daredevil: aerial walkover, kip-to-front salto, cartwheel-to-back handspring flight series, double-back salto, double-twist **dismount**. The way she held her emotions in check and exuded an otherworldly calm was

Nadia Comaneci was only in kindergarten when she first began receiving gymnastics lessons

arresting. The performance she gave at the 1976 Olympics in Montreal was groundbreaking. She was only 14, and her name was Nadia Comaneci.

Comaneci was discovered by a Romanian coach named Béla Károlyi when he saw her doing cartwheels in a schoolyard near her home of Onesti in the Carpathian Mountains. Károlyi and his wife Marta began training her when she was just seven years old, and when Comaneci was nine, she became the youngest gymnast ever to win the Romanian Nationals gymnastics title. The Károlyis pushed Comaneci and other young Romanian gymnasts hard in their training, but Comaneci, in particular, seemed to

Comaneci's unforgettable perfect 10 in 1976 set a new standard in the world of gymnastics

welcome the challenges put before her. "If somebody tells you you're perfect, why would you train harder?" she said. "Béla is honest. I don't know where he gets it, but he can terrorize you in a good way and then joke with you after."

Soon Comaneci was competing on the international level and winning. And then came the 1976 Olympics. While participating in the team portion of Olympic competition, Comaneci accomplished something no one had ever done when she scored a perfect 10 for her uneven bars routine. The moves she executed in her 27-second performance were breathtaking, and as she swung from bar to bar—giving the impression of nearly hitting the ground on two occasions—the crowd stirred and murmured. When the judges' cumulative score was flashed on the tote board, it was listed as "1.00." Comaneci's perfect 10 was so revolutionary that the scoreboard was not equipped to present it properly. Comaneci, her dark hair tied up in a ponytail with a simple pink string, calmly accepted the score with a nod and only the hint of a smile.

Comaneci would go on to record 6 more perfect 10 scores in Montreal, and she captured gold medals in the individual all-around, the uneven bars, and the balance beam while collecting a bronze medal in the floor exercise and a silver with her Romanian squadmates in the team competition. In the 1980 Olympics in Moscow, Comaneci won four more medals, two of them gold.

In the years that followed, Comaneci yearned to leave her country due to the restraints it put on her personal freedoms and the freedom of the Romanian people in general, but she was not permitted to go. In 1989, Comaneci defected to the U.S. Later, she married former Olympic gymnast Bart Conner, whom she had first met at a gymnastics event in 1976.

Comaneci was famous for her cool demeanor, appearing fearless as she pulled off daring maneuvers

ATHENS, GREECE	PARIS, FRANCE	ST. LOUIS, MISSOURI	LONDON, ENGLAND	STOCKHOLM, SWEDEN	ANTWERP, BELGIUM	PARIS, FRANCE	AMSTERDAM, NETHERLANDS	LOS ANGELES, CALIFORNIA	BERLIN, GERMANY	LONDON, ENGLAND	HELSINKI, FINLAND	MELBOURNE, AUSTRALIA	ROME, ITALY	TOKYO, JAPAN	MEXICO CITY, MEXICO	MUNICH, WEST GERMANY	MONTREAL, QUEBEC	MOSCOW, SOVIET UNION	LOS ANGELES, CALIFORNIA	SEOUL, SOUTH KOREA	BARCELONA, SPAIN	ATLANTA, GEORGIA	SYDNEY, AUSTRALIA	ATHENS, GREECE	BEIJING, CHINA	LONDON, ENGLAND
1896	1900	1904	1908	1912	1920	1924	1928	1932	1936	1948	1952	1956	1960	1964	1968	1972	1976	1980	1984	1988	1992	1996	2000	2004	2008	2012

BÉLA THE BEAR

BÉLA KÁROLYI

Béla Károlyi looked like a bear. He had a furry mustache and huge paws, and he often wrapped his tiny gymnasts in congratulatory bear hugs. He sounded like a bear, often making growling, snuffing, and roaring sounds. He even acted like a bear, sometimes dancing, sometimes charging, and sometimes pounding.

Béla Károlyi built a lofty reputation by helping coach nine different gymnasts to Olympic gold medals

Károlyi began his athletic career participating in an event that a bear—if one were able to partake in athletic competition—would likely choose. He threw the hammer in track and field and set national records in his native Romania in doing so. He also dabbled in rugby, boxing, and handball, showing promise in each sport. But when he tried gymnastics, he found out the hard way that his body wasn't gymnastically inclined when he broke his arm. He did, however, meet a woman named Marta Eross who was as obsessed about gymnastics as he was, and the two married in 1963 and began training young female gymnasts.

While Béla coached with the loud gruffness of a bear, Marta coached in a more reserved manner, showing a special talent for quietly dispensing technical advice to the gymnasts, many of whom were very young and in search of parental figures. In fact, the extreme youth of the girls under the tutelage of the Károlyis—most started training between the ages of 7 and 11— sometimes generated controversy, but the Károlyis would soon get what they wanted: their nation's best and brightest athletes intent on the highest gymnastic achievement.

In 1967, Béla happened upon a young gymnast named Nadia Comaneci, and the meeting would change his life. After training Comaneci and other young girls into their mid-teens, the Károlyis took their athletes— who made up most of Romania's national team—to the Montreal Olympics of 1976, where they captured the silver medal in team competition. Comaneci made global headlines, too, by earning the sport's first perfect 10 score there.

Soon, though, Béla began to feel mistreated by his country. When he made a scene at the 1980 Olympics in reaction to what he perceived as unbalanced judging, he was **reprimanded** by his government. In 1981, the Károlyis defected to the U.S.

Right away, the Károlyis opened a gym in America, and by 1983, they were training world-class gymnasts once again. One of those young gymnasts was Mary Lou Retton, who won all-around gold at the 1984 Olympics in Los Angeles; another was Julianne McNamara, who earned the first perfect 10 by an American female in Olympic competition. Through the end of the 20th century and beyond, the Károlyis continued to train young American gymnasts.

In 2008, Béla was asked to provide television analysis for NBC during its Olympic gymnastics broadcasts in Beijing, China. He proved to be insightful and entertaining in the role. He also proved to be as passionate about the sport as ever, nearly pummeling studio host Bob Costas into submission out of pure excitement as the two watched the gymnastics competition unfold. "I've got the bruises," said Costas. "He's a hugger. He gives you the fist in the elbow or in the shoulder." Károlyi made no apologies for his enthusiasm. If Costas had not been present, Béla said, "I'd elbow the television set. That would be my best friend."

ATHENS, GREECE — 1896
PARIS, FRANCE — 1900
ST. LOUIS, MISSOURI — 1904
LONDON, ENGLAND — 1908
STOCKHOLM, SWEDEN — 1912
ANTWERP, BELGIUM — 1920
PARIS, FRANCE — 1924
AMSTERDAM, NETHERLANDS — 1928
LOS ANGELES, CALIFORNIA — 1932
BERLIN, GERMANY — 1936
LONDON, ENGLAND — 1948
HELSINKI, FINLAND — 1952
MELBOURNE, AUSTRALIA — 1956
ROME, ITALY — 1960
TOKYO, JAPAN — 1964
MEXICO CITY, MEXICO — 1968
MUNICH, WEST GERMANY — 1972
MONTREAL, QUEBEC — 1976
MOSCOW, SOVIET UNION — 1980
LOS ANGELES, CALIFORNIA — 1984
SEOUL, SOUTH KOREA — 1988
BARCELONA, SPAIN — 1992
ATLANTA, GEORGIA — 1996
SYDNEY, AUSTRALIA — 2000
ATHENS, GREECE — 2004
BEIJING, CHINA — 2008
LONDON, ENGLAND — 2012

SKIP TO MARY LOU

1984 LOS ANGELES, CALIFORNIA

On the evening of August 3, 1984, a large and boisterous crowd filled Pauley Pavilion in Los Angeles to watch a small and boisterous American gymnast named Mary Lou Retton. Retton, a sturdy 4-foot-8 and as bubbly as a soda pop, was attempting to become the first female gymnast outside Eastern Europe to capture individual all-around Olympic gold.

Mary Lou Retton was just 16 years old when she became an American sports icon in 1984

Going into the final events, Retton's main competitor was Ecaterina Szabo of Romania. Szabo opened the finals with a perfect 10 on the balance beam, while Retton got a 9.85 on the uneven bars, leaving their cumulative scores tied at 49.375. Next, Szabo took to the mat for her floor exercise, which she performed to the American Civil War-era song "The Battle Hymn of the Republic" and received a near-perfect 9.95 score. Retton, meanwhile, scored just a 9.80 on the balance beam, leaving her .15 of a point behind Szabo. "I knew she had me edged on points," said Retton afterward. "But I also knew that I had the floor exercise and the vault coming up. And they are my strong events."

Szabo opened the door slightly when she scored an imperfect 9.90 on the vault, while Retton performed a flawless floor exercise that opened with a double back somersault in the layout position (a move considered impossible for other gymnasts at the time), closed with a dramatically perfect dismount, and garnered a perfect 10 from the judges. The effort left her just five one-hundredths of a point behind Szabo and sent the home crowd into a tizzy.

In the moments before the rivals' final event, a large, mustachioed man—who had acquired a credential to be on the main floor only as an "equipment adjuster"—stood on the sidelines giving Retton encouraging looks and words. Although he was not an official coach of the American team, he was the reason Retton was in this position. The man was Béla Károlyi, and he had once coached Retton's hero— 1976 Olympic gymnastics champion Nadia Comaneci—in his native Romania before defecting to the U.S. in 1981. In 1983, Károlyi and his wife Marta had invited Retton to move from West Virginia to their home gym in Houston, Texas. Each encouraging look from Béla seemed to buoy the tiny gymnast's confidence as the Los Angeles crowd's noise swelled following the flashing of Szabo's score on the uneven bars: 9.90.

Retton approached the vault runway and waved to the crowd. A perfect 10 would win it all. Then, her eyes went steely as she eyed the vault table some 80 feet away. With a hop, Retton was off, streaking toward the apparatus. She sprang, hit the table, did a layout back somersault with a twist—another nearly impossible move—and nailed her landing. The score was a perfect 10. "I knew I had it," said Retton of her legendary vault, which secured gold. "Listen, I knew by my run that I had it. I knew it when I was in the air."

In 1985, a year after her triumphant Games, Retton was inducted into the U.S. Olympic Hall of Fame

ATHENS, GREECE 1896
PARIS, FRANCE 1900
ST. LOUIS, MISSOURI 1904
LONDON, ENGLAND 1908
STOCKHOLM, SWEDEN 1912
ANTWERP, BELGIUM 1920
PARIS, FRANCE 1924
AMSTERDAM, NETHERLANDS 1928
LOS ANGELES, CALIFORNIA 1932
BERLIN, GERMANY 1936
LONDON, ENGLAND 1948
HELSINKI, FINLAND 1952
MELBOURNE, AUSTRALIA 1956
ROME, ITALY 1960
TOKYO, JAPAN 1964
MEXICO CITY, MEXICO 1968
MUNICH, WEST GERMANY 1972
MONTREAL, QUEBEC 1976
MOSCOW, SOVIET UNION 1980
LOS ANGELES, CALIFORNIA 1984
SEOUL, SOUTH KOREA 1988
BARCELONA, SPAIN 1992
ATLANTA, GEORGIA 1996
SYDNEY, AUSTRALIA 2000
ATHENS, GREECE 2004
BEIJING, CHINA 2008
LONDON, ENGLAND 2012

MAGNIFICENT TRIUMPH

1996 ATLANTA, GEORGIA

The 1996 U.S. women's gymnastics team had great expectations. The squad's three 19-year-olds—Shannon Miller, Dominique Dawes, and Amanda Borden—were the leaders of a tight-knit team. Miller was considered America's most talented gymnast, having won five Olympic medals in Barcelona in 1992, including a silver in the individual all-around. Dawes was a solid all-around performer who

Béla Károlyi carrying an injured Kerri Strug became the defining image of the 1996 Games

became the first African American gymnast (along with teammate Betty Okino) to win an Olympic medal when the U.S. took bronze in the 1992 team competition. Borden was the most outspoken and encouraging member of the team, having been unanimously voted team captain by the other members of the group.

Other U.S. gymnasts included 18-year-old Amy Chow, a wonder on the uneven bars; 18-year-old Kerri Strug, a shy but fierce competitor who excelled in the vault; 16-year-old Jaycie Phelps, a hard worker who had overcome serious injuries to compete in Atlanta; and Dominique Moceanu, a spunky 15-year-old who charmed audiences and judges alike with her spirited floor routines. The group's official coaches were Marta Károlyi and Mary Lee Tracy, though Béla Károlyi and Steve Nunno were the more outspoken coaches barking from the sidelines in Atlanta, even if their coaching titles were deemed "unofficial."

Dubbed "The Magnificent Seven" by the American media, Team USA got off to a great start in the team competition as it sought to claim team gold for the first time. One by one, the American girls drew high scores and

In the 1996 Games, Shannon Miller became America's most decorated gymnast ever by winning the sixth and seventh medals of her Olympic career.

thunderous applause from the 32,000 fans who packed the Georgia Dome to watch the competition. And then, suddenly, the gymnasts in stars and stripes began to falter. Particularly devastating to America's chances for gold was a fall by Moceanu in the vault that registered a low score. The spotlight turned on Strug in the Americans' final vault. She would have to score a 9.493 to clinch the gold. "The Russians, I knew, were on the floor, which can be a high-scoring event, and my heart was beating like crazy," said Strug. "I thought, 'This is it, Kerri. You've done this vault a thousand times.'"

Strug's first vault was a disaster. Under-rotating, she landed hard, heard her ankle pop, and fell. The judges scored it a 9.162. Worse, her ankle was injured. In a dramatic moment that would change her life, Strug had to decide whether to press forward with her final vault at the risk of further injury. She decided to do it. Strug took to the vault's runway, executed the

The Magnificent Seven: (from left) Dawes, Moceanu, Strug, Chow, Phelps, Borden, and Miller.

vault—landing mostly on one leg—and raised her arms as the crowd went wild. Strug then collapsed to the mat and was assisted to the sidelines. The judges rated the vault a 9.712, the American women captured the gold, and Béla Károlyi—in an iconic moment—cradled the injured Strug in his arms and carried her to the medal stand.

Throughout the national anthem, Strug cried tears of both joy and pain. Her ankle injury forced her to pull out of individual competition in the Games, but she was a hero. "In my 35 years of coaching, I have never seen such a moment," Károlyi said of Strug's feat. "People think these girls are fragile dolls. They're not. They're courageous."

The women's team gold was 1 of 44 gold medals won by U.S. Olympians in the Atlanta Games

1896	1900	1904	1908	1912	1920	1924	1928	1932	1936	1948	1952	1956	1960	1964	1968	1972	1976	1980	1984	1988	1992	1996	2000	2004	2008	2012
ATHENS, GREECE	PARIS, FRANCE	ST. LOUIS, MISSOURI	LONDON, ENGLAND	STOCKHOLM, SWEDEN	ANTWERP, BELGIUM	PARIS, FRANCE	AMSTERDAM, NETHERLANDS	LOS ANGELES, CALIFORNIA	BERLIN, GERMANY	LONDON, ENGLAND	HELSINKI, FINLAND	MELBOURNE, AUSTRALIA	ROME, ITALY	TOKYO, JAPAN	MEXICO CITY, MEXICO	MUNICH, WEST GERMANY	MONTREAL, QUEBEC	MOSCOW, SOVIET UNION	LOS ANGELES, CALIFORNIA	SEOUL, SOUTH KOREA	BARCELONA, SPAIN	ATLANTA, GEORGIA	**SYDNEY, AUSTRALIA**	ATHENS, GREECE	BEIJING, CHINA	LONDON, ENGLAND

A LOW HORSE AND LOST GOLD

2000 SYDNEY, AUSTRALIA

Something was definitely wrong with the women's vault apparatus in Sydney at the 2000 Olympics. One by one, gymnasts botched their performances—first in warm-ups, then in official competition.

American Amy Chow vaulting in the 2000 Games—an event that turned unexpectedly dangerous

Elise Ray of the U.S. nearly missed the vaulting horse altogether in warm-ups, coming down violently on her back as a result. "It really scared me," said Ray, who then also fell on both of her official vaults to score a disappointing 7.618.

Annika Reeder of Great Britain took such a tumble on the vault that she was injured and had to withdraw from further competition. Svetlana Khorkina of Russia, 5-foot-5 and willowy by gymnastics standards, was considered by many to be the all-around favorite for gold, but when she tried a vault, she landed on her knees. The 9.343 score she received so disturbed her that she botched her subsequent uneven bars routine, falling again and receiving a low score. Only when Allana Slater, an Australian gymnast, complained to meet officials about the horse did officials look into the matter—when Khorkina had made an inquiry earlier, she had been ignored. To the officials' horror, it was discovered that the horse had been set at 120 centimeters instead of the standard 125 centimeters. The gymnasts had been vaulting on a horse that was set five centimeters (two inches) too low.

When the gymnasts found out about the error, some were irate, even though those who vaulted on the lowered horse were given a chance to retry their vaults. "I'm disappointed, but I'm also angry," said Ray, "and I'm sure the other competitors feel the same way." Khorkina definitely felt the same anger, saying, "It was cruel to all the participants to vault on a nonstandard height. It's quite possible to get killed. The five centimeters could decide the future of a sports person."

Audiences and experts were equally confounded by the error. "It's incredible," said Bart Conner, a former U.S. gymnast covering the Sydney Games as a commentator. "Setting the vault at the wrong height doesn't happen even in 10-year-old age group trials. The one thing that saved the

Andreea Raducan captured—and then lost—individual all-around gold in 2000, her only Olympiad

credibility of the meet is that Andreea Raducan won. She's so good, she could win anytime."

Raducan, a Romanian spark plug in the mold of the legendary Nadia Comaneci, performed on the faulty vault without falling and captured all-around gold. Unfortunately, her victory was marred—and ultimately erased—when a drug test showed that she had a drug called pseudoephedrine in her system. Raducan's coaches had given her two cold medicine pills prior to competition without realizing they contained banned substances. As a result, Raducan was stripped of her all-around gold medal. Even after an appeal at the Court of Arbitration for Sport in Switzerland, the decision to take away Raducan's gold was upheld. The gold medal went, then, to Raducan's teammate Simona Amanar. "For me, the medal doesn't mean anything," said Amanar. "I'm going to accept it because it belongs to Romania. But I didn't win it. The Olympic champion that day was Andreea, not me."

After the 2000 Games, Simona Amanar returned the individual all-around gold to Andreea Raducan.

ATHENS, GREECE | PARIS, FRANCE | ST. LOUIS, MISSOURI | LONDON, ENGLAND | STOCKHOLM, SWEDEN | ANTWERP, BELGIUM | PARIS, FRANCE | AMSTERDAM, NETHERLANDS | LOS ANGELES, CALIFORNIA | BERLIN, GERMANY | LONDON, ENGLAND | HELSINKI, FINLAND | MELBOURNE, AUSTRALIA | ROME, ITALY | TOKYO, JAPAN | MEXICO CITY, MEXICO | MUNICH, WEST GERMANY | MONTREAL, QUEBEC | MOSCOW, SOVIET UNION | LOS ANGELES, CALIFORNIA | SEOUL, SOUTH KOREA | BARCELONA, SPAIN | ATLANTA, GEORGIA | SYDNEY, AUSTRALIA | **ATHENS, GREECE** | BEIJING, CHINA | LONDON, ENGLAND

1896 | 1900 | 1904 | 1908 | 1912 | 1920 | 1924 | 1928 | 1932 | 1936 | 1948 | 1952 | 1956 | 1960 | 1964 | 1968 | 1972 | 1976 | 1980 | 1984 | 1988 | 1992 | 1996 | 2000 | **2004** | 2008 | 2012

TARNISHED MEDAL

2004 ATHENS, GREECE

In 2004 in Athens, Russian gymnast Alexei Nemov was participating in his third and final Olympics. He was a popular athlete, known as much for his death-defying, circus-like aerial maneuvers as the 12 medals he had won in previous Olympic competition. In the finals of the horizontal bar competition in Athens, the 28-year-old veteran of an inexperienced Russian team seemed to be at

Alexei Nemov's showmanship and highflying moves made him a fan favorite in three Games

his best. Nemov flawlessly executed six highflying and treacherous release moves, drawing *oohs* and *ahhs* from the crowd. Although his dismount—a flashy double flip with a spinning twist—was slightly marred by a heavy forward step on the landing, the fans went wild at his performance. The judges didn't seem so impressed. Nemov was given a 9.725 cumulative score. The crowd immediately began to boo, whistle, and shout at what it deemed an unfairly low score.

Nearby, American gymnast Paul Hamm readied for his turn on the high bar, but the crowd's vocal disapproval continued to the extent that Hamm couldn't concentrate. "I was telling myself to focus because it was so

The adjustment of Nemov's score from its original 9.725 made for a controversial scene in 2004

distracting," said Hamm. "I had never heard the crowd that loud in my life. It almost seemed like a movie or something." As a result of the disturbance, Hamm decided to take a seat and wait things out.

Meanwhile, the judges began conferring. The minutes dragged on until, suddenly, Nemov's score was reposted as a 9.762. The Malaysian judge had raised her score for Nemov from 9.60 to 9.75, and the Canadian judge also raised his score to 9.75 from the previous 9.65. "I've never seen that done before," said U.S. assistant coach Myles Avery. "It's highly, highly unusual. To change scores because of crowd noise? What it says about gymnastics is not very good." Although Nemov's score was corrected, he remained out of medal contention in the event. He did, however, appear before the crowd after nearly 15 minutes' time and raised his hands to quiet its protests so that Hamm could continue. Nemov's gesture was appreciated by the Americans, who referred to him as an upholder of the Olympic spirit.

The judges' blunders were not finished. In the all-around competition, they failed to correctly assess the difficulty level of South Korean gymnast Yang Tae Young, which resulted in his score being unfairly lowered. If it had been corrected, Yang would have bumped the declared winner—Hamm—from the top spot by 0.051 of a point. Hamm, who had thought his performance had given him the first male all-around gold in American Olympic history, was deeply disappointed by the controversy. At the request of the South Korean team, the matter was eventually taken to the Court of Arbitration for Sport, where Hamm's gold was upheld. "This medal means a lot, even more now than it did in the past, because we had to fight so hard for it," said Hamm after the ruling. "I feel like I won it three times—in the competition, in the media, and also in court. It's probably the most sought-after medal of all the Olympic Games ever."

Paul Hamm had an identical twin named Morgan, and both brothers competed on the U.S. team in the 2000 and 2004 Olympics. Injuries prevented the Hamms from participating in the 2008 Games.

Paul Hamm fell on the vault in Athens but scored well enough in the five other events to win all-around gold

ATHENS, GREECE   1896
PARIS, FRANCE   1900
ST. LOUIS, MISSOURI   1904
LONDON, ENGLAND   1908
STOCKHOLM, SWEDEN   1912
ANTWERP, BELGIUM   1920
PARIS, FRANCE   1924
AMSTERDAM, NETHERLANDS   1928
LOS ANGELES, CALIFORNIA   1932
BERLIN, GERMANY   1936
LONDON, ENGLAND   1948
HELSINKI, FINLAND   1952
MELBOURNE, AUSTRALIA   1956
ROME, ITALY   1960
TOKYO, JAPAN   1964
MEXICO CITY, MEXICO   1968
MUNICH, WEST GERMANY   1972
MONTREAL, QUEBEC   1976
MOSCOW, SOVIET UNION   1980
LOS ANGELES, CALIFORNIA   1984
SEOUL, SOUTH KOREA   1988
BARCELONA, SPAIN   1992
ATLANTA, GEORGIA   1996
SYDNEY, AUSTRALIA   2000
ATHENS, GREECE   2004
BEIJING, CHINA   2008
LONDON, ENGLAND   2012

THE CHINESE TAKEOVER

2008 BEIJING, CHINA

With China hosting the Olympics for the first time in history in 2008, expectations for Chinese athletes to win medals were extremely high. For the Chinese men's gymnastics team, expectations were through the roof, since it had won the team Olympic gold just eight years earlier in Sydney before

Backed by the loud support of the home crowd, Jiang Yuyuan finished fourth in the floor exercise in Beijing

finishing a disappointing fifth in 2004. Back from the championship Chinese team were top gymnasts Huang Xu, Yang Wei, and Li Xiaopeng.

After the 2004 Olympic gymnastics competition—which had been marred by several judging blunders—the International Gymnastics Federation (FIG) made major changes to the traditional scoring system, which had formerly been based on a 10-point system. Under the new "code of scoring," judges gave scores that usually fell in the 14- to 16-point range, with a flawless routine perhaps earning a 17, and routines that were more daring and had a higher degree of difficulty were rewarded over the simple absence of mistakes. Romanian-American coach Béla Károlyi echoed the sentiments of many of the old guard when he said, "Why take the perfect 10 out? It was so understandable. It was our trademark. It gave us such visibility and recognition."

The team gold in men's gymnastics contributed to an Olympics-best 51 gold medals for China in 2008

For Chinese gymnasts in 2008, the new system seemed fine. In men's competition, Yang Wei led his mates to gold in the team competition and won the all-around individual title, and Yang's teammates dominated the other individual events, winning gold in all of them except the vault, which went to Polish gymnast Leszek Blanik. In women's competition, China also won team gold with a stable of small and daring young dynamos.

Upon further review, however, it seemed the Chinese girls may have been *too* small and *too* young. Media reports surfaced suggesting that four of the Chinese gymnasts—He Kexin, Yang Yilin, Jiang Yuyuan, and Deng Linlin—did not meet the minimum age requirement of 16. (The minimum had been raised from 15 to 16 in 1997.) "We heard these rumors, and we immediately wrote to the Chinese gymnastics federation," said Andre Gueisbuhler, FIG secretary general. "They immediately sent a copy of the passport, showing the age, and everything is okay. That's all we can check." Other veteran coaches weren't convinced that China was being honest. Károlyi said that coaches had forever been trying to fool officials into letting underage girls compete, since younger girls—who are usually lighter and more flexible—can do some physical maneuvers that older and "stiffer" gymnasts cannot. Károlyi cited as an example a North Korean gymnast with missing front teeth at the 1991 world championships, whom he placed at about 11 years old. North Korea had listed the gymnast as being 15 years old for 3 straight years and was later banned by the FIG.

The 2008 Games would not be China's last run-in with an underage gymnast controversy. In 2010, the International Olympic Committee (IOC) stripped medals from a female Chinese gymnast named Dong Fangxiao. Dong had competed in 2000 in Sydney as an alleged 17-year-old, though facts later surfaced proving that she was actually 14. In the case of the 2008 Games, though, accusations remained only that, and China celebrated a near sweep of gymnastics glory.

After winning gold in Beijing, the Chinese women's team was a favorite going into the London Games

ATHENS, GREECE	PARIS, FRANCE	ST. LOUIS, MISSOURI	LONDON, ENGLAND	STOCKHOLM, SWEDEN	ANTWERP, BELGIUM	PARIS, FRANCE	AMSTERDAM, NETHERLANDS	LOS ANGELES, CALIFORNIA	BERLIN, GERMANY	LONDON, ENGLAND	HELSINKI, FINLAND	MELBOURNE, AUSTRALIA	ROME, ITALY	TOKYO, JAPAN	MEXICO CITY, MEXICO	MUNICH, WEST GERMANY	MONTREAL, QUEBEC	MOSCOW, SOVIET UNION	LOS ANGELES, CALIFORNIA	SEOUL, SOUTH KOREA	BARCELONA, SPAIN	ATLANTA, GEORGIA	SYDNEY, AUSTRALIA	ATHENS, GREECE	BEIJING, CHINA	LONDON, ENGLAND
1896	1900	1904	1908	1912	1920	1924	1928	1932	1936	1948	1952	1956	1960	1964	1968	1972	1976	1980	1984	1988	1992	1996	2000	2004	2008	2012

THE GAMES OF 2012

The 2012 Olympics were to be held in London, England. Londoners got the news in July 2005, and as is the case any time an Olympic host is selected, city and national officials sprang into action. Although seven years may seem to be plenty of time for preparation, it is in fact a small window when one considers that host cities typically need to create housing for thousands of

In 2012, London was to play host to its third Summer Olympiad, having done so in 1908 and 1948

international athletes and coaches (generally in a consolidated area known as the "Athletes' Village"), expand public transportation options (such as trains and buses), and build outdoor playing fields, indoor arenas, and other venues with enough seating—and grandeur—to be worthy of Olympic competition.

The numbers involved in the 2012 Games indicate just how large a venture it is to host an Olympiad. Some 10,500 athletes from 200 countries were to compete in London, with 2,100 medals awarded. About 8 million tickets were expected to be sold for the Games. And before any athletes arrived or any medals were awarded, it was anticipated that the total cost of London's Olympics-related building projects and other preparations would approach $15 billion.

Among those construction projects was the creation of Olympic Park, a sprawling gathering area in east London that was to function as a center of activity during the Games. From the park, people would be able to move to numerous athletic facilities in and around the city. Those facilities included the 80,000-seat Olympic Stadium, which was built to host track and field events as well as the opening and closing ceremonies; the new Basketball Arena, a temporary structure that was to be dismantled after the Games; and the $442-million Aquatics Centre, which was designed both to host swimming events and to serve as a kind of visitors' gateway to Olympic Park. Other notable venues included the North Greenwich Arena (which was to host gymnastics), the ExCeL center (boxing), Earls Court (indoor volleyball), and Horse Guards Parade (beach volleyball).

In July 2011, British prime minister David Cameron and IOC president Jacques Rogge reviewed all preparations and proudly declared that the city was nearly ready to welcome the world. "This has the makings of a great British success story," Cameron announced. "With a year to go, it's on time, it's on budget.... We must offer the greatest ever Games in the world's greatest country."

Rogge kicked off the one-year countdown to the Games by formally inviting countries around the world to send their greatest athletes to the British capital in 2012. "The athletes will be ready," said Rogge. "And so will London."

apparatus — in gymnastics, the equipment used by gymnasts in competition; it includes the balance beam, horizontal bar, pommel horse, parallel bars, rings, uneven bars, and vaulting horse

balance beam — a long, narrow, elevated beam on which female gymnasts perform routines demonstrating exceptional balance; the beam is 1.25 meters high and measures 5 meters long by 10 centimeters wide

certified — confirmed as being genuine or official

compatriots — people from the same country

defected — deserted one's own country—usually because of poor conditions or mistreatment—in a permanent move to another country

dismount — in gymnastics, the act of concluding a routine or event by leaping or dropping from an elevated apparatus

floor exercise — a gymnastics event in which gymnasts execute a sequence of tumbles, flips, and poses on a spring-supported floor measuring 12 meters by 12 meters

horizontal bar — a bar positioned 2.5 meters off the ground on which male gymnasts perform balancing moves, revolutions, releases, and changes of direction before dismounting; it is sometimes called the high bar

innovators — people who use or show new and creative methods or ideas

layout — describing an aerial maneuver or position in which a gymnast's body is straight, without any bend in the legs or hips

parallel bars — two parallel bars on which male gymnasts perform swinging, balancing, and vaulting maneuvers; the bars are positioned 2 meters off the ground and 42 to 52 centimeters apart

pommel horse — a padded apparatus attached to the floor with two handles on top, on which male gymnasts perform spinning and balancing maneuvers while touching the apparatus only with their hands

preliminary — leading up to the main event; preliminary events serve to narrow a field of athletes to only the best competitors

reprimanded — given a harsh and official showing of disapproval, usually by a higher authority

rings — two rings that descend from straps attached to a higher metal frame that are used by male gymnasts to perform swinging and balancing routines and to demonstrate upper-body strength; they are sometimes called still rings

stereotypical — describing a formulaic or oversimplified vision of a group of people, events, or issues

unanimously — showing complete and absolute agreement

uneven bars — two bars on which female gymnasts perform revolutions, balancing moves, releases, and transitions from bar to bar before dismounting; the bars are set 1.3 to 1.8 meters apart at heights of 2.41 meters and 1.61 meters

vault — a gymnastics event in which gymnasts sprint down a runway, jump off a springboard, and launch off a vaulting horse, performing various twists and turns in the air before landing on their feet

vaulting horse — a padded gymnastics apparatus attached to the floor; gymnasts sprint to it and spring off it using their hands in the vault competition

Selected Bibliography

Anderson, Dave. *The Story of the Olympics*. New York: HarperCollins, 2000.

Guttmann, Allen. *The Olympics: A History of the Modern Games*. Urbana: University of Illinois Press, 2002.

MacCambridge, Michael, ed. *SportsCentury*. New York: ESPN, 1999.

Macy, Sue, and Bob Costas. *Swifter, Higher, Stronger: A Photographic History of the Summer Olympics*. Washington, D.C.: National Geographic, 2008.

Maraniss, David. *Rome 1960: The Olympics That Changed the World*. New York: Simon & Schuster, 2008.

Osborne, Mary Pope. *Ancient Greece and the Olympics*. New York: Random House, 2004.

Sullivan, James E., ed. *Spalding's Official Athletic Almanac*. New York: American Sports Publishing, 2010.

Walters, Guy. *Berlin Games: How the Nazis Stole the Olympic Dream*. New York: William Morrow, 2006.

Web Sites

International Olympic Committee
www.olympic.org
This site is the official online home of the Olympics and features profiles of athletes, overviews of every sport, coverage of preparation for the 2012 Summer Games, and more.

Sports-Reference / Olympic Sports
www.sports-reference.com/olympics
This site is a comprehensive database for Olympic sports and features complete facts and statistics from all Olympic Games, including medal counts, Olympic records, and more.

INDEX

Published by Creative Education
P.O. Box 227, Mankato, Minnesota 56002
Creative Education is an imprint of
The Creative Company
www.thecreativecompany.us

Design and production by The Design Lab
Art direction by Rita Marshall

Printed by Corporate Graphics in
the United States of America

Photographs by Alamy (Mary Evans Picture
Library, Keystone Pictures USA, Eileen Langsley
Gymnastics), American Numismatic Society,
Getty Images (AFP/AFP, AFP, Natalie Behring/
Bloomberg, Clive Brunskill, ADRIAN DENNIS/
AFP, Stu Forster, IOP/AFP, NY Daily News, Doug
Pensinger /Allsport, Doug Pensinger, E Phillips,
Mike Powell/Allsport, Steve Powell, Ezra Shaw
/Allsport, Ezra Shaw, Sports Illustrated, Bob
Thomas, Al Tielemans /Sports Illustrated),
Dreamstime (Alain Lacroix), iStockphoto (ray
roper), Missouri History Museum, St. Louis,
Shutterstock (rook76)

Library of Congress
Cataloging-in-Publication Data
LeBoutillier, Nate.
Gymnastics / by Nate LeBoutillier.
p. cm. — (Summer Olympic legends)
Summary: A survey of the highlights and
legendary athletes—such as Romanian
Nadia Comaneci—of the Olympic sport of
gymnastics, which has been part of the
modern Summer Games since 1896.
Includes bibliographical references and index.
ISBN 978-1-60818-210-7
1. Gymnasts—Biography—Juvenile literature.
2. Gymnastics—Juvenile literature. 3. Olympics—
Juvenile literature. I. Title.
GV460.L43 2012
796.44—dc23   2011032496

CPSIA: 030111 PO 1452

First Edition
9 8 7 6 5 4 3 2 1